English 6-7
Handwriting

Lynn Huggins-Cooper

Contents

2 Information for parents
4 Daffodil writes letters
6 Clover goes Moo!
8 Sebastian eats grass
10 Candy makes soup
12 Fun time!
14 Terence visits friends
16 Daffodil eats pie
18 Princess looks and learns
20 Gus falls over
22 Horace shares with friends
24 Fun time!
26 Henrietta loves babies

28 Gus watches spiders
30 Cheeky, Cheery and Chirpy have a snack
32 Clover plans a picnic
34 Fun time!
36 Henrietta chases chicks
38 Sebastian gets cold feet
40 Horace harvests wheat
42 Daffodil looks around
44 Princess plays hide and seek
46 Answers
48 Goodbye!

Information for parents

This book is designed to help your child to develop a cursive or 'joined' writing style. The activities will encourage them to practise writing individual joins and whole words. You could also ask your child to watch as you write, so they can see the actual joins flowing. Try to make sure your child makes the joins correctly from the beginning (rather than just creating the shapes in any way he or she can) as this will help them to develop an easy, relaxed cursive writing style.

The development of handwriting is part of the National Curriculum for 6–7 year olds. Do not be concerned if your child is working at a higher or lower level than some of the activities. All children develop at their own pace. You know your child and their capabilities best, so be guided by them. If they find something difficult, come back to it later – they may not be ready.

Do not carry out activities that are beyond them, as they will become frustrated. Once the activities become a chore, you will find it difficult to encourage your child to get involved and engage with the book. Instead, fit the activities into your usual day. When you are carrying out the activities in this book, try to make sure your child has quiet time, free from distractions such as the television. Make sure you are relaxed too and not in a hurry or distracted. Give your child your full attention and they will enjoy the 'together time'. If learning is fun, your child will be eager for more!

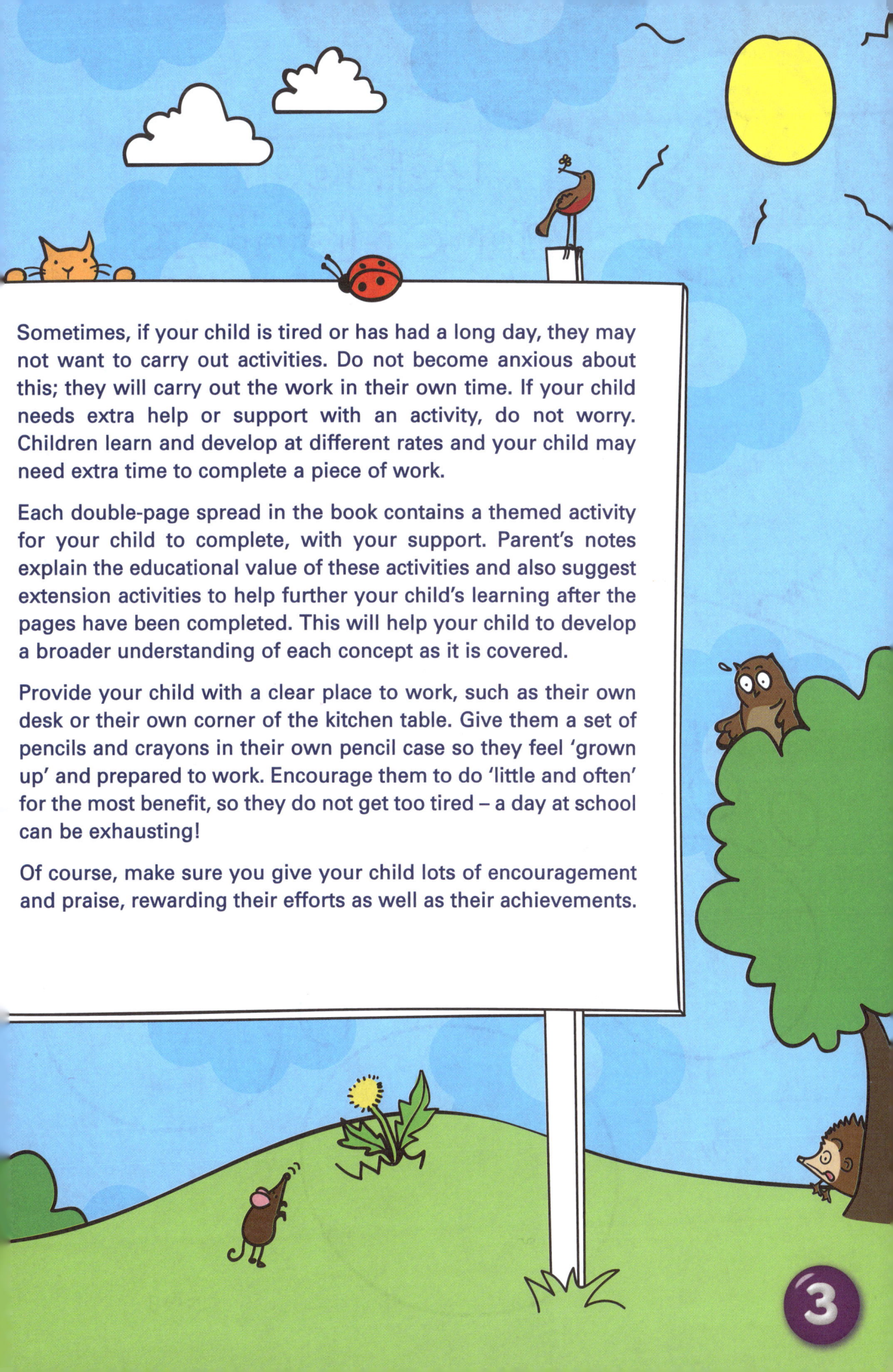

Sometimes, if your child is tired or has had a long day, they may not want to carry out activities. Do not become anxious about this; they will carry out the work in their own time. If your child needs extra help or support with an activity, do not worry. Children learn and develop at different rates and your child may need extra time to complete a piece of work.

Each double-page spread in the book contains a themed activity for your child to complete, with your support. Parent's notes explain the educational value of these activities and also suggest extension activities to help further your child's learning after the pages have been completed. This will help your child to develop a broader understanding of each concept as it is covered.

Provide your child with a clear place to work, such as their own desk or their own corner of the kitchen table. Give them a set of pencils and crayons in their own pencil case so they feel 'grown up' and prepared to work. Encourage them to do 'little and often' for the most benefit, so they do not get too tired – a day at school can be exhausting!

Of course, make sure you give your child lots of encouragement and praise, rewarding their efforts as well as their achievements.

Now have a go at writing the whole alphabet on the side of the barn!

Parent's note
This activity encourages your child to look closely at the shape of letters. Give her lots of opportunity to practise. Make 26 cards and ask your child to write the letters of the alphabet on them. She can then sort them into piles of 'short', 'tall' and 'tail' letters.

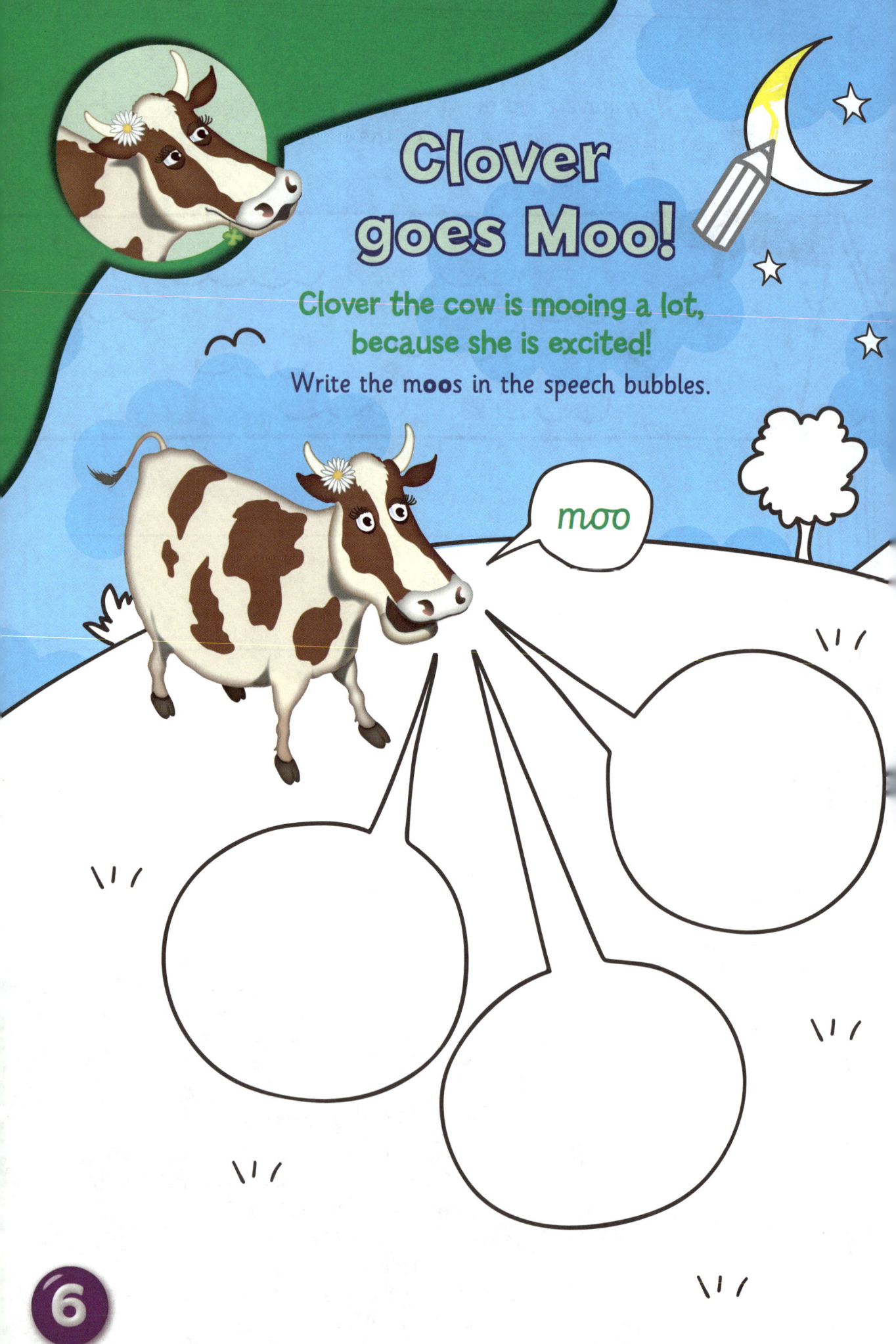

Now Clover is talking to her friends. Copy the things she says onto the lines below.

"Look at the moon!"

"Seb shook his woolly coat."

"Who will cook me some food?"

Now practise writing a line of **oo**s.

oo oo

Parent's note
This activity will help your child to form the join **oo**. All the joins in this book should be written in cursive (joined-up) handwriting. Example joins can be found on the right hand side of every spread.

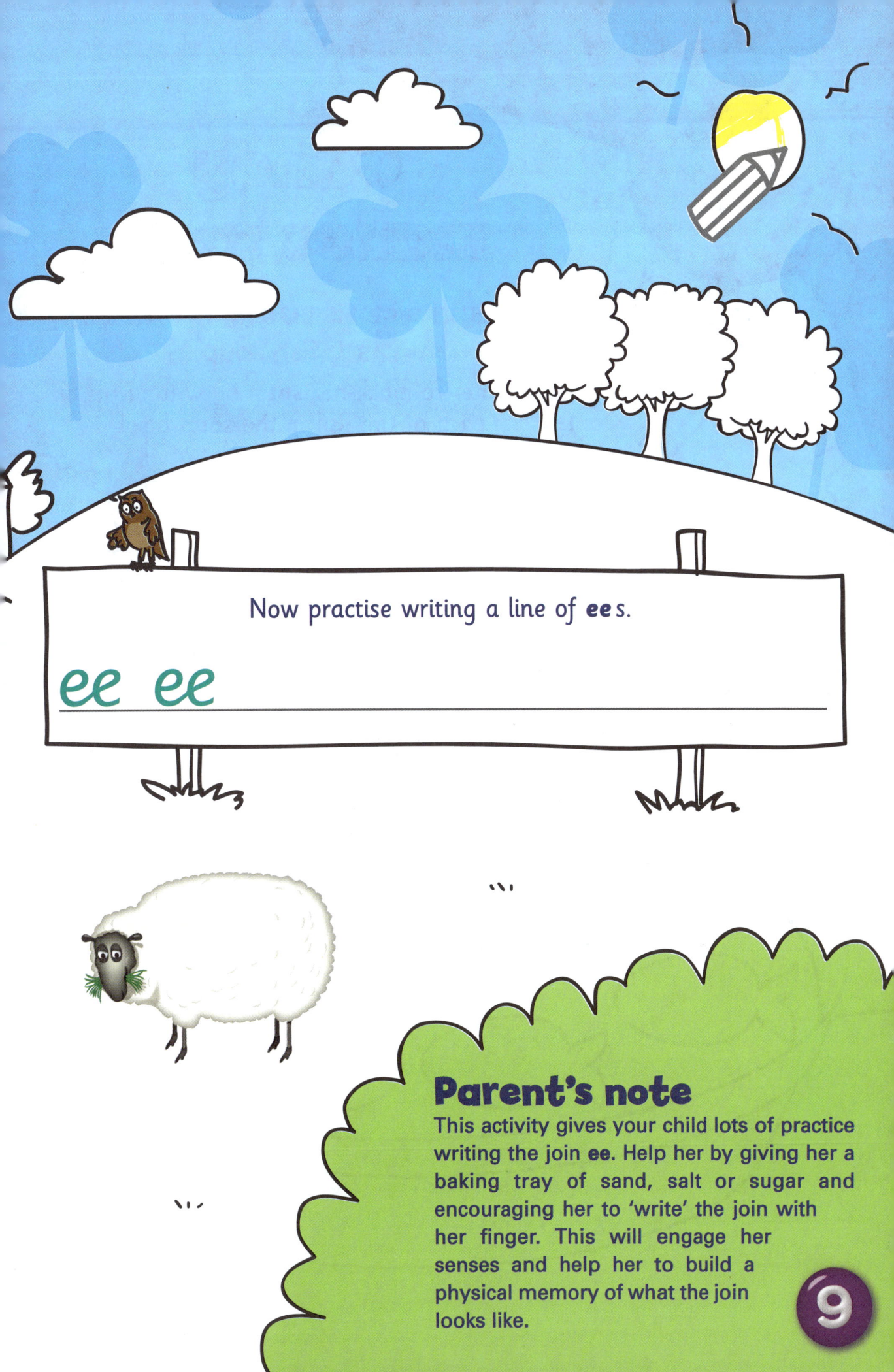

Now practise writing a line of **ou**s.

ou ou

Parent's note
This activity will help your child to form the rounded letters **o** and **u** as the letter string **ou**. Make sure your child is sitting comfortably as she writes, as she is more likely to be relaxed and write neatly.

Fun time!

Join the dots to find out which Fun Farmyard friends are playing by the pond.

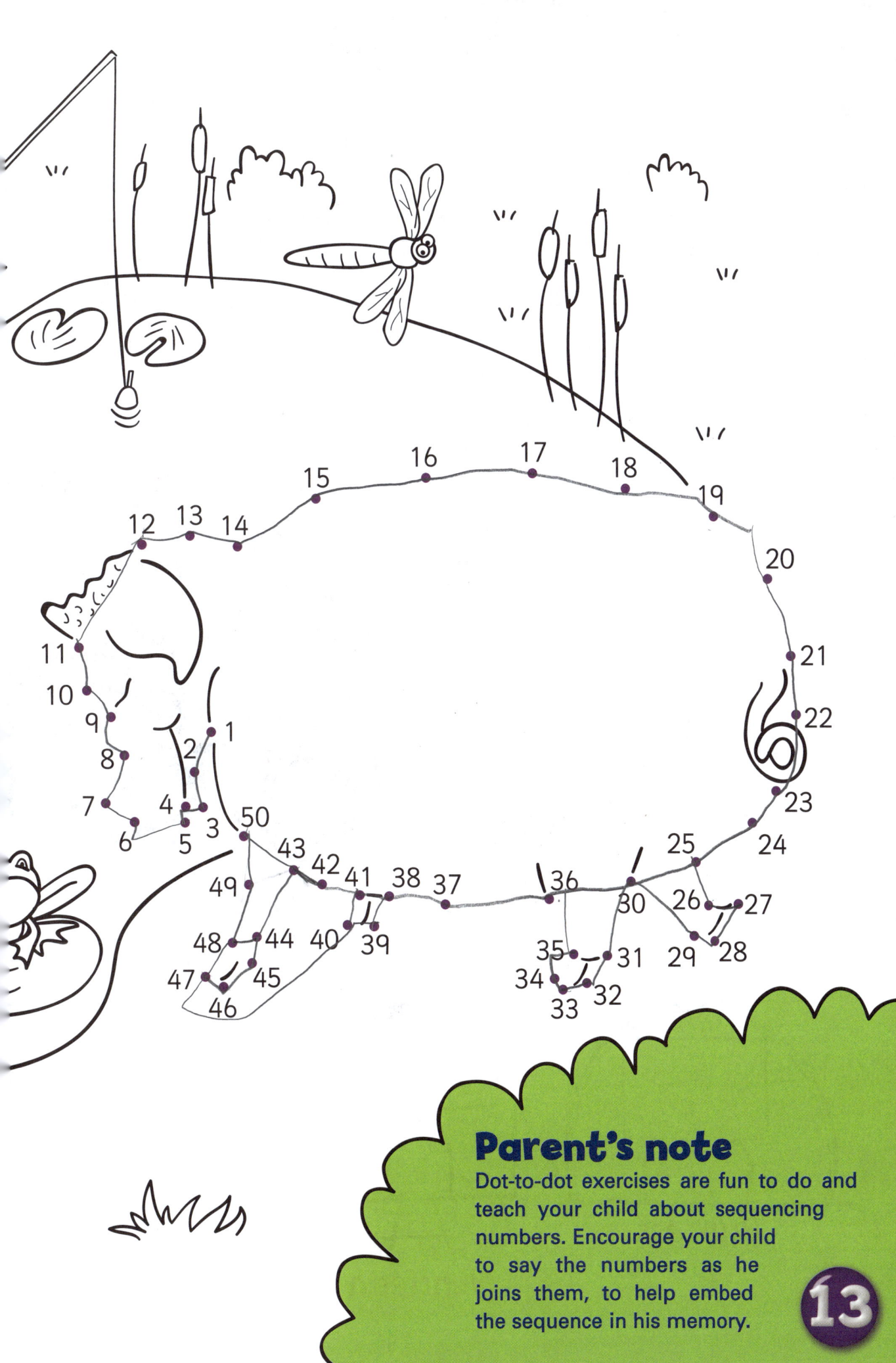

Parent's note
Dot-to-dot exercises are fun to do and teach your child about sequencing numbers. Encourage your child to say the numbers as he joins them, to help embed the sequence in his memory.

13

Practise writing a line of **om**s.

om om

Now practise writing a line of **on**s. They are like **om**s!

on on

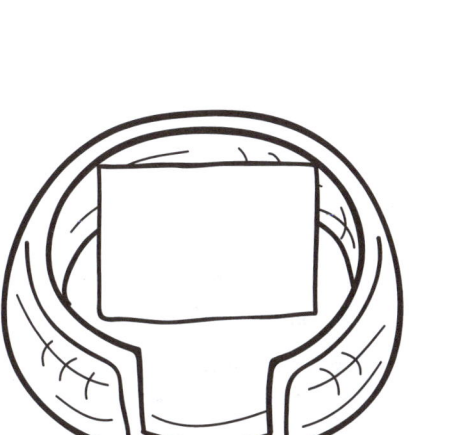

Candy

Parent's note
This activity helps your child to make the common joins **om** and **on**. Encourage your child to practise the join for **om** and **on** at the same time, as they are so similar.

Now practise writing a line of **vi**s and **wi**s.

vi vi

wi wi

Parent's note
These joins are very similar. Encourage your child to practise them together, so she recognises the similarity. Writing large letters with chalk on a board will help her to form the letters correctly.

Practise writing a line of **at**s.

at at

Now practise writing a line of **it**s.

it it

Parent's note
This activity joins a short letter to a tall letter. Help your child to ensure that there is enough difference in size between the short and tall letters. Young children often find this difficult. It may be worth ruling 'double lines' for your child on a piece of paper so he can see where to stop the short letter (halfway between lines) and where to finish the tall letter.

Fun time!

Here's the home of the Fun Farmyard friends in summer. Why don't you colour it in?

Parent's note
Colouring in is not just a time filler. It supports the development of fine motor skills in your child's hands and fingers. These skills will help her to hold pencils and crayons, and this will benefit her writing and drawing skills.

Gus watches spiders

Gus the goat is watching his pet spiders spin webs between the bells on the farmhouse door.

Watch with him. Write **et** on the p**et** spiders, **eb** on the w**eb**s and **el** on the b**el**ls.

Now practise writing a line of **et**s, **eb**s and **el**s.

et et

eb eb

el el

Parent's note
This activity gives your child the opportunity to write more 'tall and short' letter combinations. Writing these three joins together is helpful, because they all start with the letter **e**. As your child forms the letters, encourage her to give a commentary – 'around, up and down' for the **el** pattern, for example. This will help her to remember the sequence of pencil movements that creates the correct join.

Practise writing a line of **ut**s.

ut ut

Now practise writing a line of **ul**s.

ul ul

Parent's note
Encourage your child to make a collection of **ut** and **ul** words by cutting them out of magazines and newspapers. Your child can stick them on a sheet of paper and write the words underneath in cursive joined-up script.

Fun time!

Look at these two pictures of Clover the cow.
They look the same – but are they?

There are 15 differences between the pictures. Draw a circle round each difference you find.

Parent's note

'Spot the difference' activities help to build observational skills and a longer concentration span. You could also play the memory game, where your child looks at a tray of objects which is then covered and your child tries to recall them, to further develop these areas.

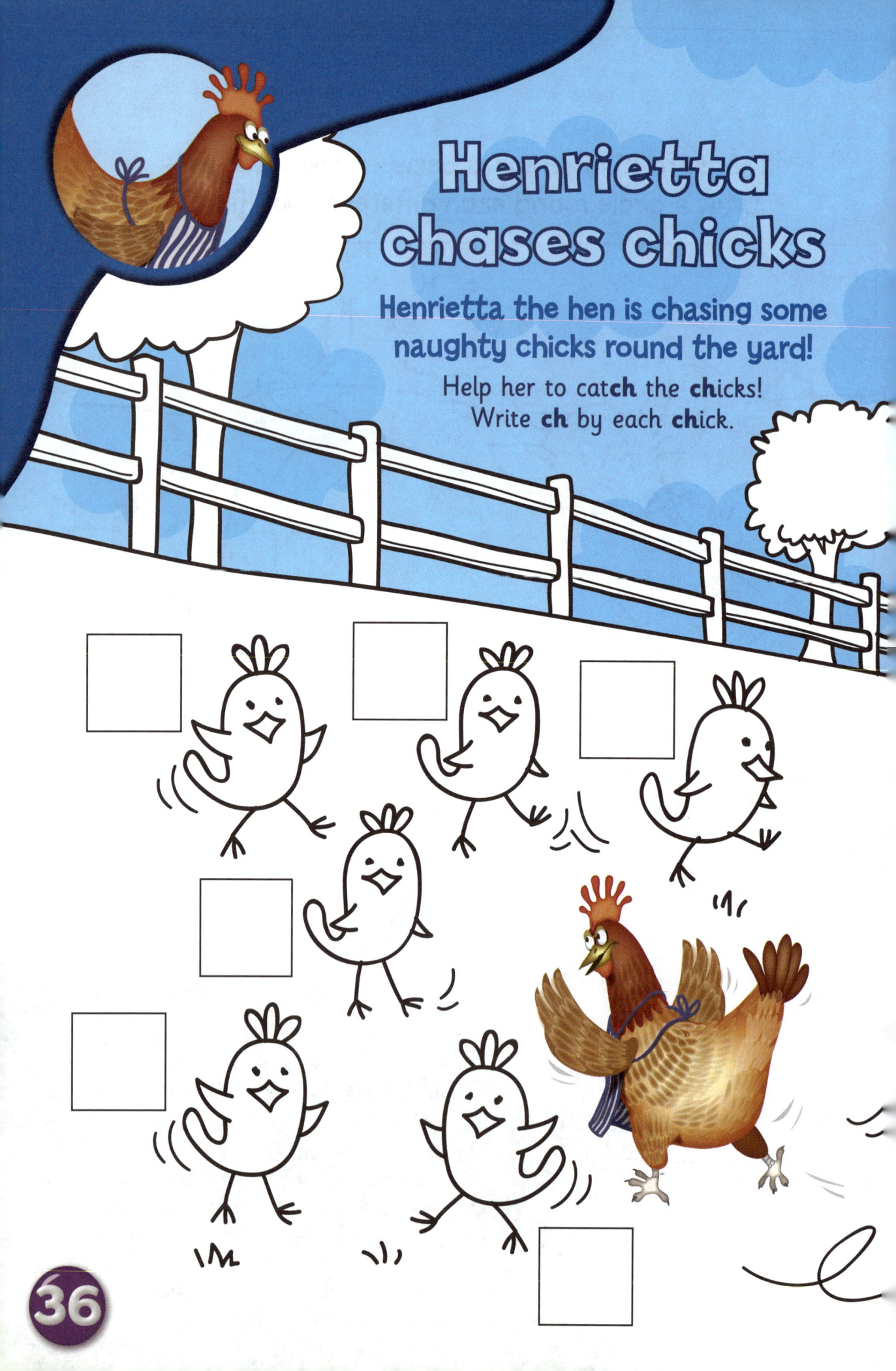

Now practise writing a line of **ch**s.

ch ch

Parent's note
Help your child to write the join **ch** by writing the shape and encouraging him to watch. Trace the shape together in a tray of sand or sugar, to build a sensory memory of the join shape.

37

Sebastian gets cold feet

Sebastian the sheep and his friends have holes in their woolly socks! They need to thread their needles so they can sow up the holes.

Help **th**em to **th**read **th**eir needles.
Write **th** on each sheep.

Now practise writing a line of **th**s.

th th

Parent's note
Help your child to write the pattern **th**, keeping the **t** slightly shorter than the **h**. Encourage him to write regularly – it really is a case of 'practice makes perfect'.

39

Horace harvests wheat

Horace the horse is moving the bundles of wheat as they are harvested.

Help him to move the **wh**eat by writing **wh** on the bundles.

Now practise writing a line of **wh**s.

wh wh _____

Parent's note
Look for words that begin with **wh** together. Question words – what, where, when, why – are a good start! Encourage your child to write them in large format on scrap paper.

41

Daffodil looks around

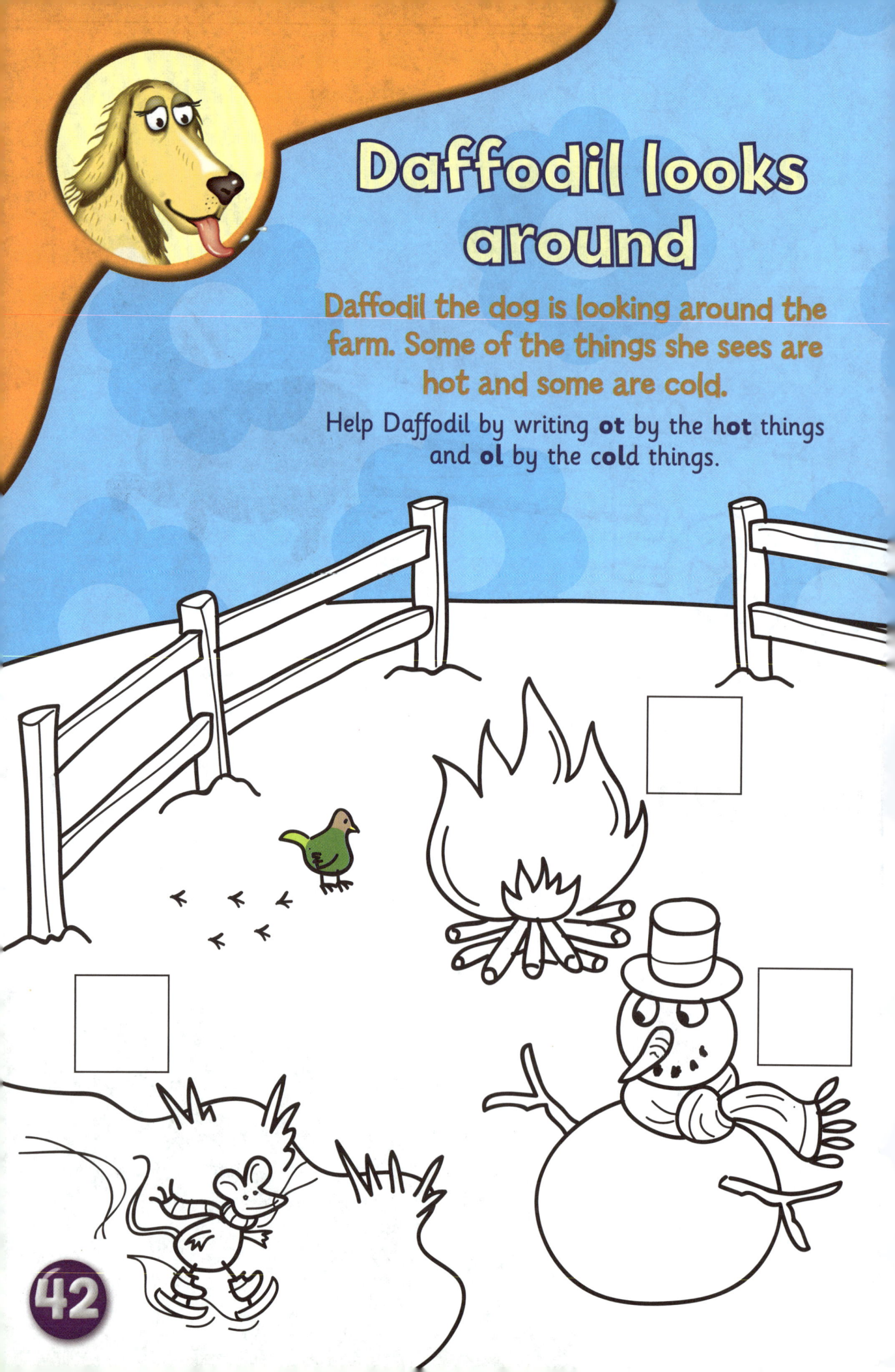

Daffodil the dog is looking around the farm. Some of the things she sees are hot and some are cold.

Help Daffodil by writing **ot** by the **hot** things and **ol** by the **cold** things.

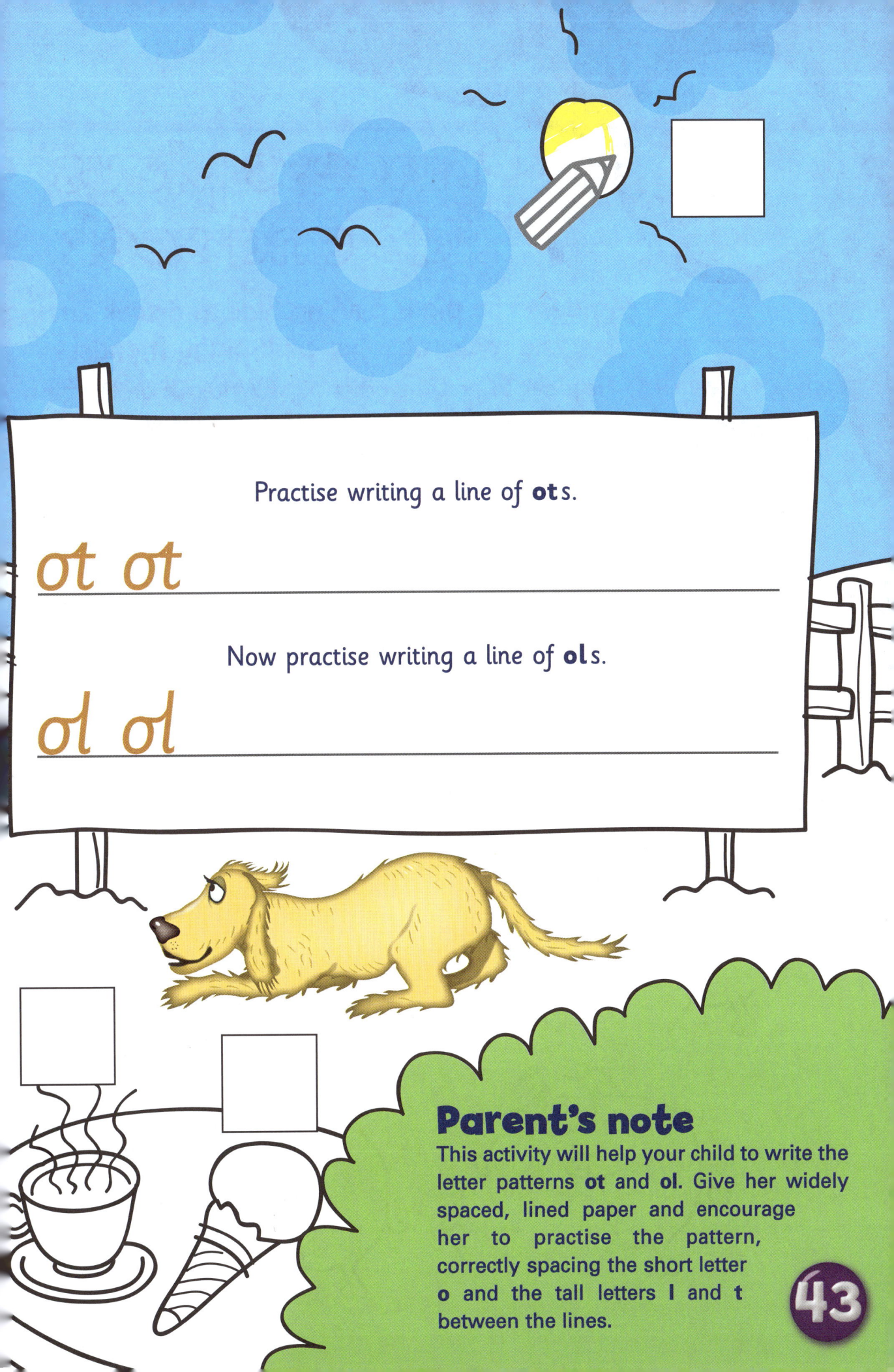

Practise writing a line of **ot**s.

ot ot

Now practise writing a line of **ol**s.

ol ol

Parent's note
This activity will help your child to write the letter patterns **ot** and **ol**. Give her widely spaced, lined paper and encourage her to practise the pattern, correctly spacing the short letter **o** and the tall letters **l** and **t** between the lines.

43

Princess plays hide and seek

Princess the pig is playing hide and seek among the rocks with her pink piggy friends!

Help her to find the other pigs. Write **nk** on the pi**nk** pigs and **ck** on the ro**ck**s they are hiding behind!

Practise writing a line of **nk**s.

nk nk

Now practise writing a line of **ck**s.

ck ck

Parent's note
nk and **ck** are quite difficult joins to master. Help your child by writing the patterns with a dry-wipe marker on a cheap wipe-clean board and encouraging your child to trace over them.

45

Answers

Pages 4–5

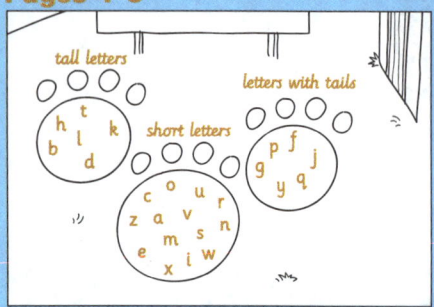

Pages 6–7
Correctly formed **moo** written in each speech bubble.

"Look at the moon!" copied correctly onto the appropriate line.

"Seb shook his woolly coat." copied correctly onto the appropriate line.

"Who will cook me some food?" copied correctly onto the appropriate line.

Correctly formed **oo**s copied onto the line.

Pages 8–9
Correctly formed **ee** written on the sheep and clumps of grass.

Correctly formed **ee**s copied onto the line.

Pages 10–11
Correctly formed **ou** written on the fish.
Correctly formed **ou**s copied onto the line.

Pages 12–13

Pages 14–15
Correctly formed **om** written on Horace's home.

Correctly formed **om** written on Princess' home.

Correctly formed **om** written on Henrietta's home.

Correctly formed **om** written on Daffodil's home.

Correctly formed **om** written on Candy's home.

Correctly formed **om**s and **on**s copied onto the lines.

Pages 16–17
Correctly formed **ve** written on the square tins.

Correctly formed **ie** written on the round tins.

Correctly formed **ve**s and **ie**s copied onto the lines.

Pages 18–19
Correctly formed **vi** written on the vine leaves.

Correctly formed **wi** written on the wine bottles.

Correctly formed **vi**s and **wi**s copied onto the lines.

Pages 20–21
Correctly formed **ng** written on the tears.

Correctly formed **ng** written on the hankies.

Correctly formed **ng**s copied onto the line.

Pages 22–23
Correctly formed **at** written on the bags of oats.

Correctly formed **it** written on the bluetits.

Correctly formed **at**s and **it**s copied onto the lines.

Pages 24–25
Picture coloured in as neatly as possible.

Pages 26–27
Correctly formed **al** written on the foals.
Correctly formed **ab** written on the other babies.

Correctly formed **al**s and **ab**s copied onto the lines.

Pages 28–29
Correctly formed **et** written on the pet spiders.
Correctly formed **eb** written on the webs.
Correctly formed **el** written on the bells.

Correctly formed **et**s, **eb**s and **el**s copied onto the lines.

Pages 30–31
Correctly formed **ut** written on the cut bags.
Correctly formed **ul** written on the full bags.

Correctly formed **ut**s and **ul**s copied onto the lines.

Pages 32–33
Correctly formed **sh** written on the dishes.
Correctly formed **st** written on the tree stumps.

Correctly formed **sh**s and **st**s copied onto the lines.

Pages 34–35

Pages 36–37
Correctly formed **ch** written on the chicks.

Correctly formed **ch**s copied onto the line.

Pages 38–39
Correctly formed **th** written on the sheep.

Correctly formed **th**s copied onto the line.

Pages 40–41
Correctly formed **wh** written on the stacks of wheat.

Correctly formed **wh**s copied onto the line.

Pages 42–43
Correctly formed **ot** written by the cup of tea, sun and fire.
Correctly formed **ol** written by the frozen pond, snowman and ice cream.

Correctly formed **ot**s and **ol**s copied onto the lines.

Pages 44–45
Correctly formed **nk** written on the pink pigs.
Correctly formed **ck** written on the rocks.

Correctly formed **nk**s and **ck**s copied onto the lines.

47

Goodbye!

Just colour us in before you go.